"Prayer is a way offered by the
Holy Spirit to reach God"
ACIM, S-1, I, 1

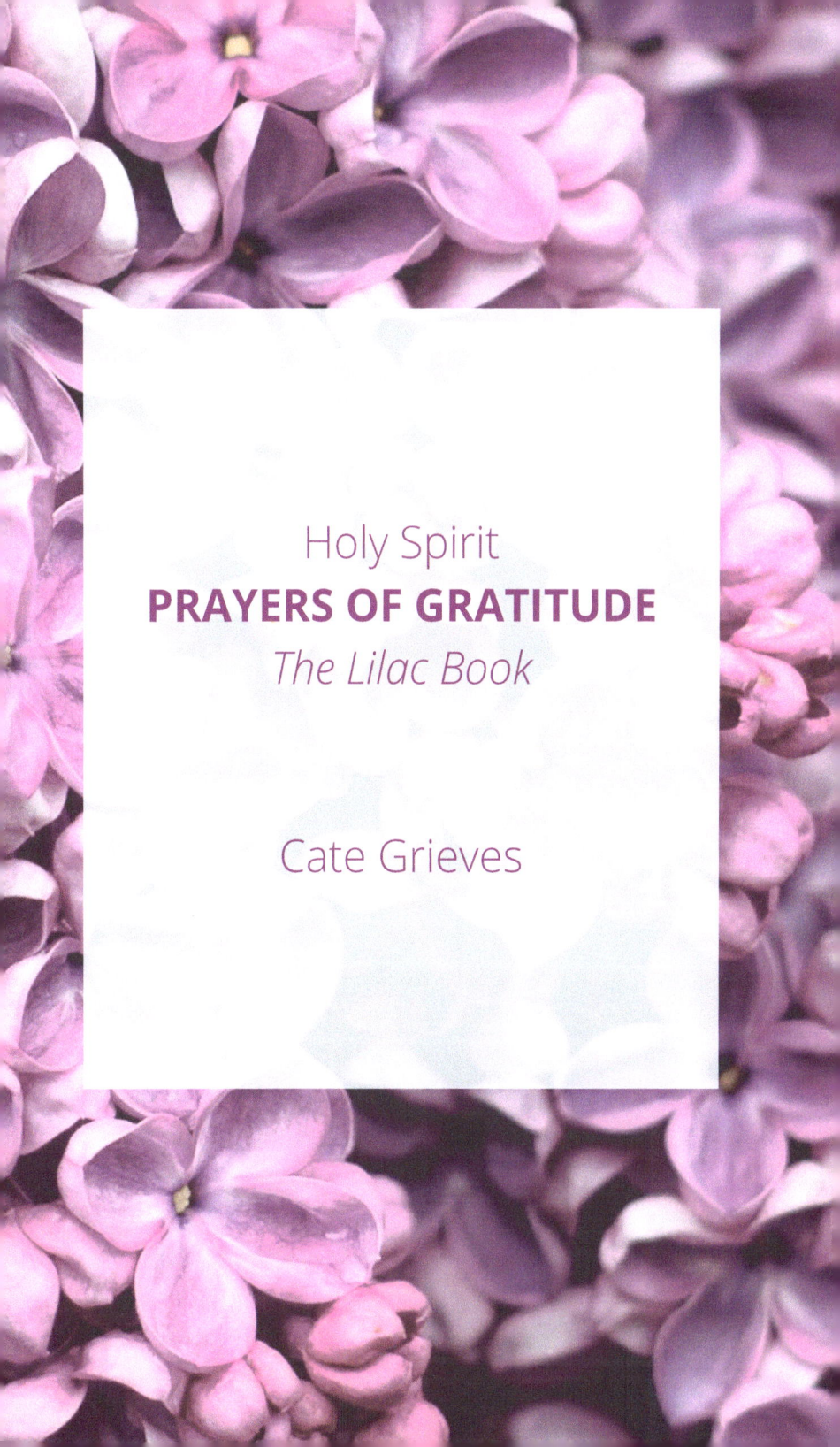

Holy Spirit
PRAYERS OF GRATITUDE
The Lilac Book

Cate Grieves

All quotes are from *A Course in Miracles* (ACIM), copyright ©1992, 1999, 2007 by the Foundation for Inner Peace, 448 Ignacio Blvd., #306, Novato, CA 94949, www.acim.org and info@acim.org, used with permission.

We would like to express gratitude for the Foundation for Inner Peace.

This is a key for the quote references:
T = Text
W = Workbook for Students
M = Manual for Teachers
C = Clarification of Terms
S = The Song of Prayer Pamphlet
P = Psychotherapy Pamphlet

ISBN 978-0-6456605-1-7

Copyright © 2022 by Cate Grieves. All rights reserved.

Designed by: Shannon Williams
Cover and interior photography: Unsplash.com

First Edition: December 2022

Blessings, Friend

Welcome, my beautiful brother. We are One in God's Mind of Infinite Love now. I welcome you to these Holy Spirit Prayers that help foster an experience of gratitude. Each prayer has been divinely gifted from the Holy Spirit to help our mind become aligned with the experience of gratitude. Each prayer has an element of inviting Him in, asking for His help and offering gratitude for what is already given. The Holy Spirit's perception is the miracle that brings forth the wisdom, love and peace that replaces the false beliefs we made up ourselves. Please read each prayer very slowly and stay with each line in silence. Feel yourself willing to let the words be the prayer of your heart.

"Truth will correct all errors in my mind." W-107

Love,

Cate

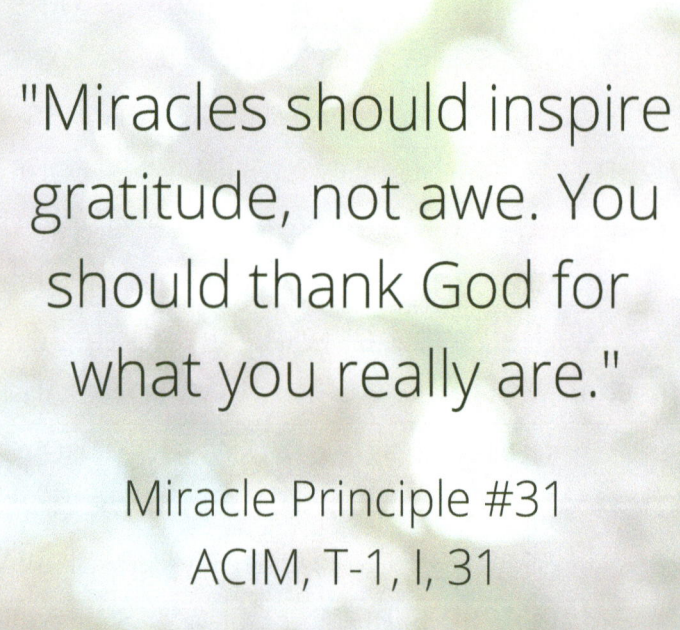

"Miracles should inspire gratitude, not awe. You should thank God for what you really are."

Miracle Principle #31
ACIM, T-1, I, 31

Holy Spirit

I join with you today

I appreciate your Presence

I give thanks to your guidance

I give thanks and joy

to your loving wisdom

I am humble to your love

I am here to be your loving servant

Which is the most joyful job I do

I desire to serve

I let go of thoughts of my body

I give it to you to use today

For Your Holy Purpose

I am here to be in service only to you

Lord, here I am

Amen

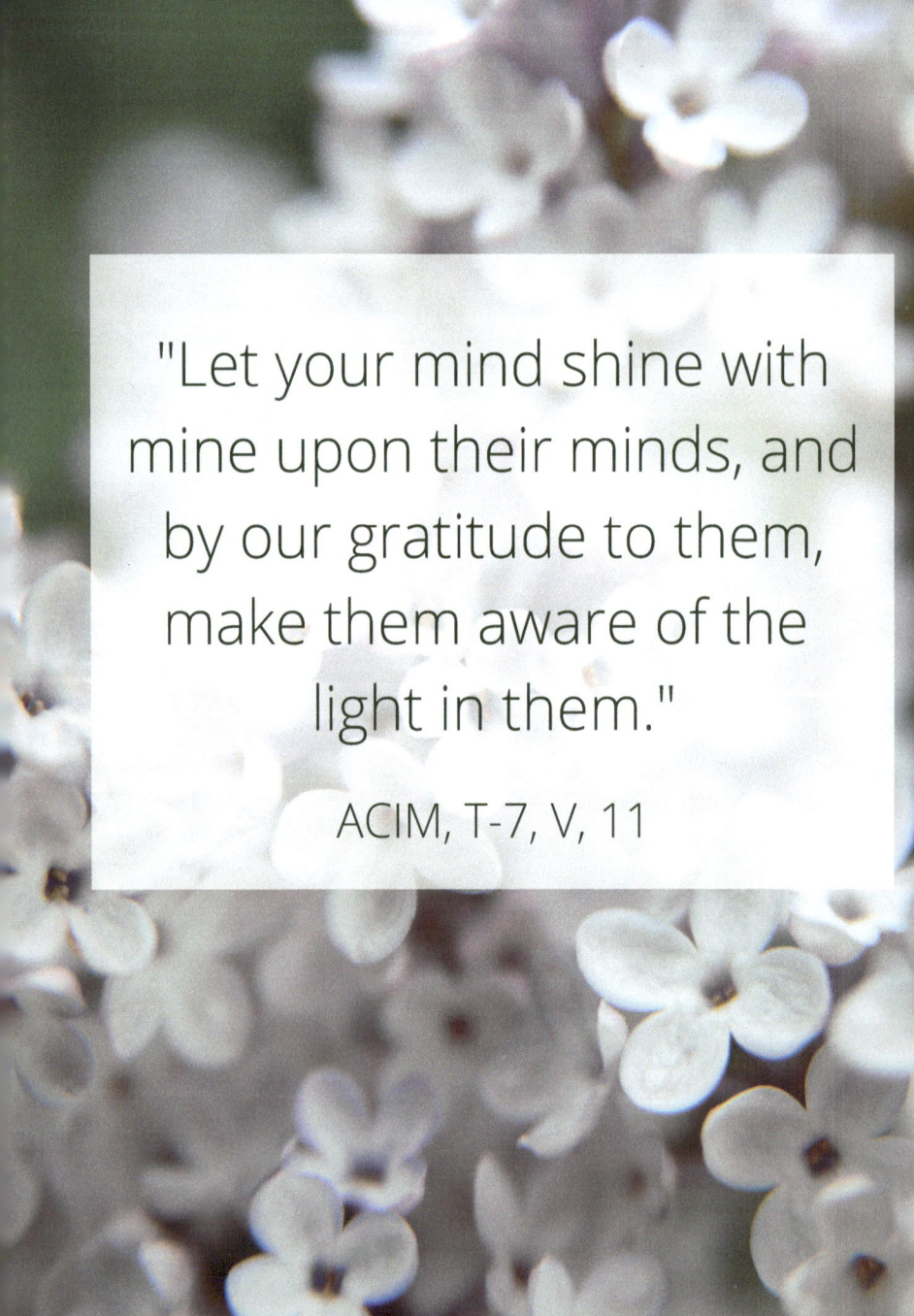

"Let your mind shine with mine upon their minds, and by our gratitude to them, make them aware of the light in them."

ACIM, T-7, V, 11

Holy Spirit

Please help me remain in
A state of blessing and gratitude
I desire only to bless
My holy brothers today

This blessing of gratitude
Washes away all thoughts of nothingness
And restores my mind
To its rightful place
In holy Innocence

I want only this
Today and every day
Amen

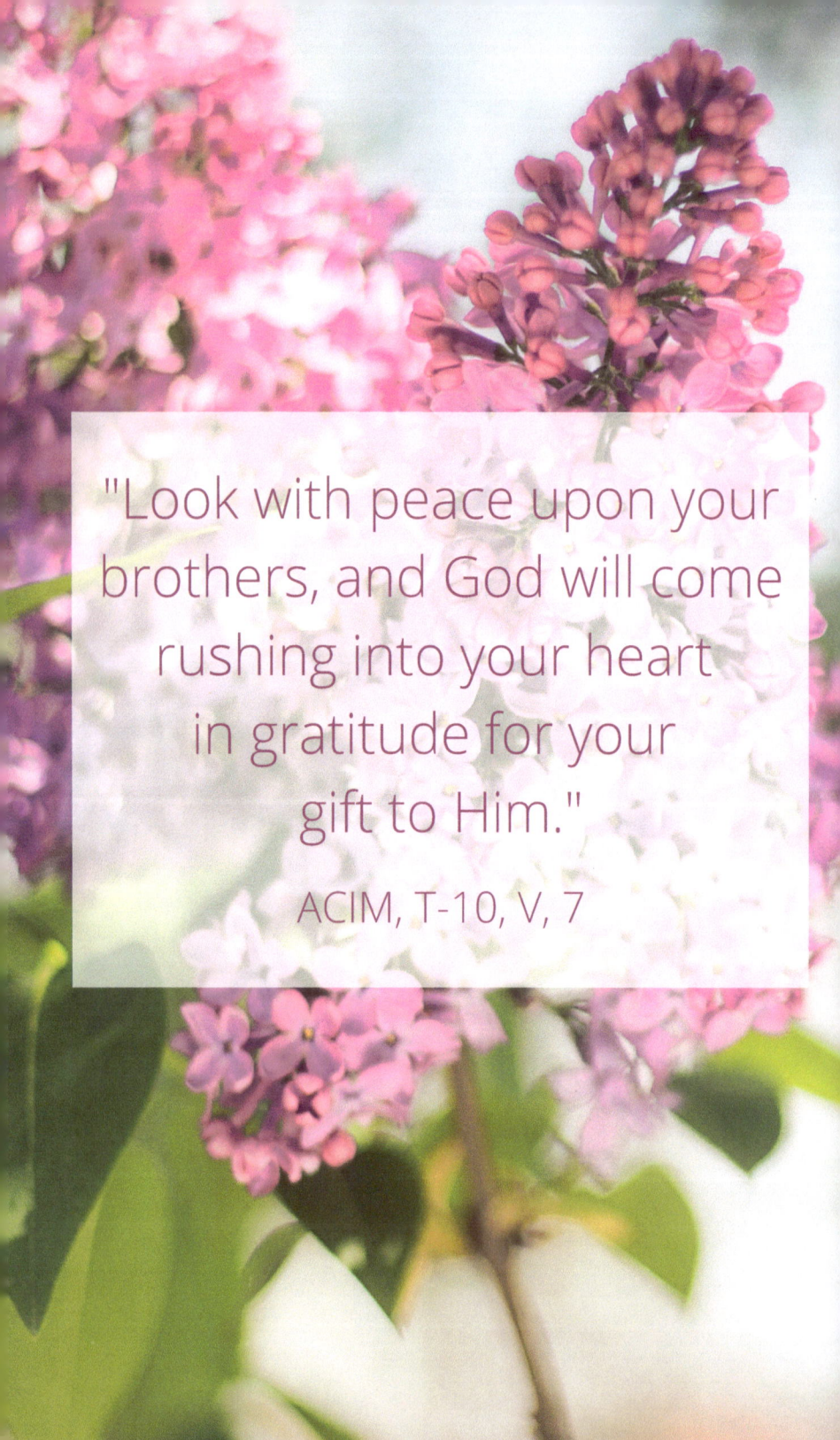

"Look with peace upon your brothers, and God will come rushing into your heart in gratitude for your gift to Him."

ACIM, T-10, V, 7

Thank you, Holy Spirit

For being my right mind

For being the light in which I see

For being with me always

For being the Holy Instant

In which I see differently

Thank you for helping me to see

My brother as he is

The Perfect Christ

In all his glory

Amen

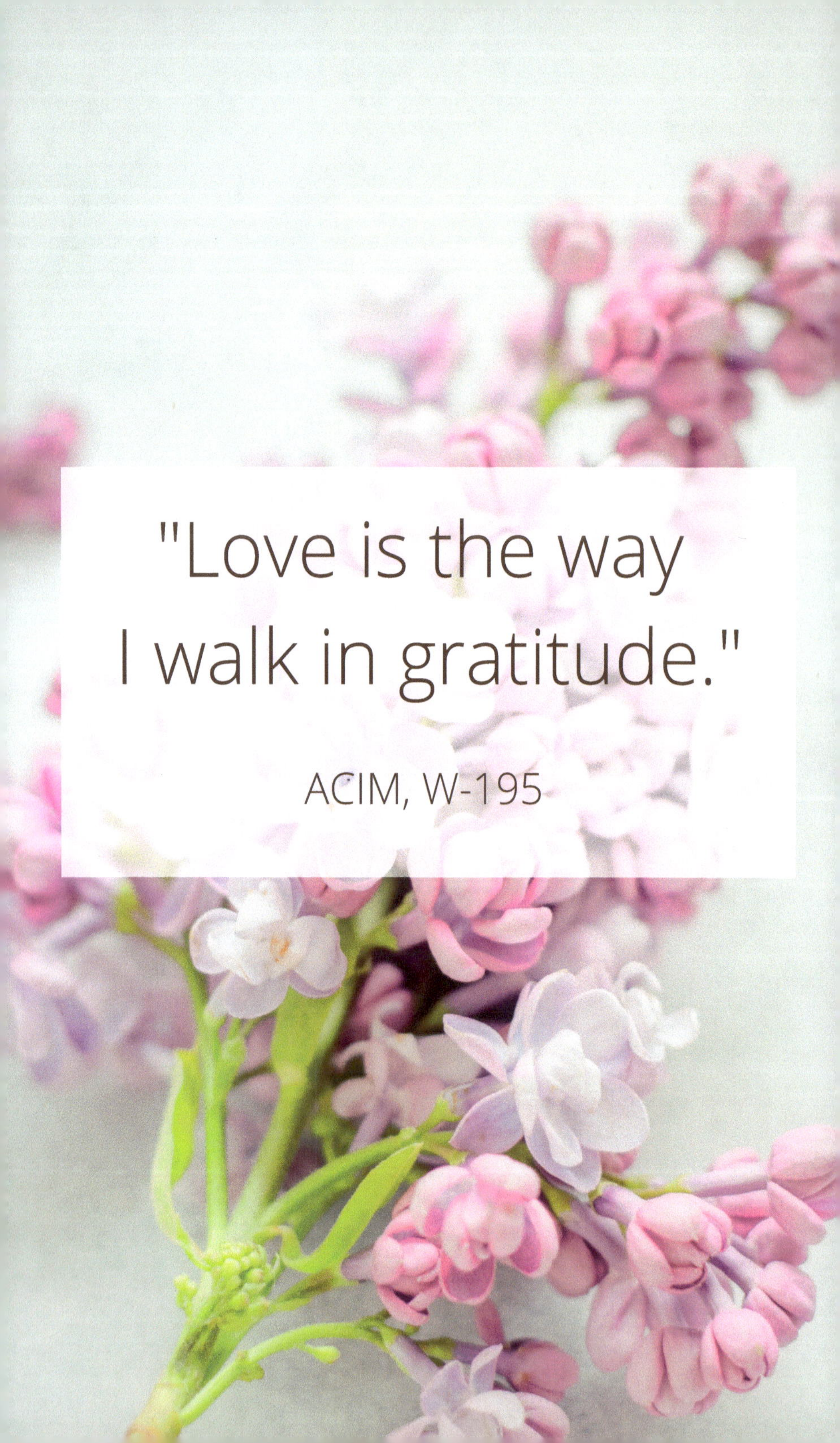

"Love is the way
I walk in gratitude."

ACIM, W-195

Holy Spirit

I give thanks today

For every living thing

For otherwise, I offer thanks for nothing

And fail to recognise the gifts of God to me

Today, I walk in gratitude

As a way of love

And let hatred be forgotten

I desire to lay aside all comparisons

And desire only to have my forgiveness complete

Illuminated in my mind

Be You in charge

Amen

"We sing the song of thankfulness today, in honor of the Self that God has willed to be our true Identity in Him."

ACIM, W-123, 4

HOLY SPIRIT

I am truly grateful today

For all that you give to me

I acknowledge that I have everything

In the beingness of You

Use me as an instrument of thy Peace

As I spend my day

Joining the Will of God

I desire

To join with your Will today

To follow Your Will

To not decide for myself

But walk with the gratitude and Love

Within me and let it naturally

Extend through me

Amen

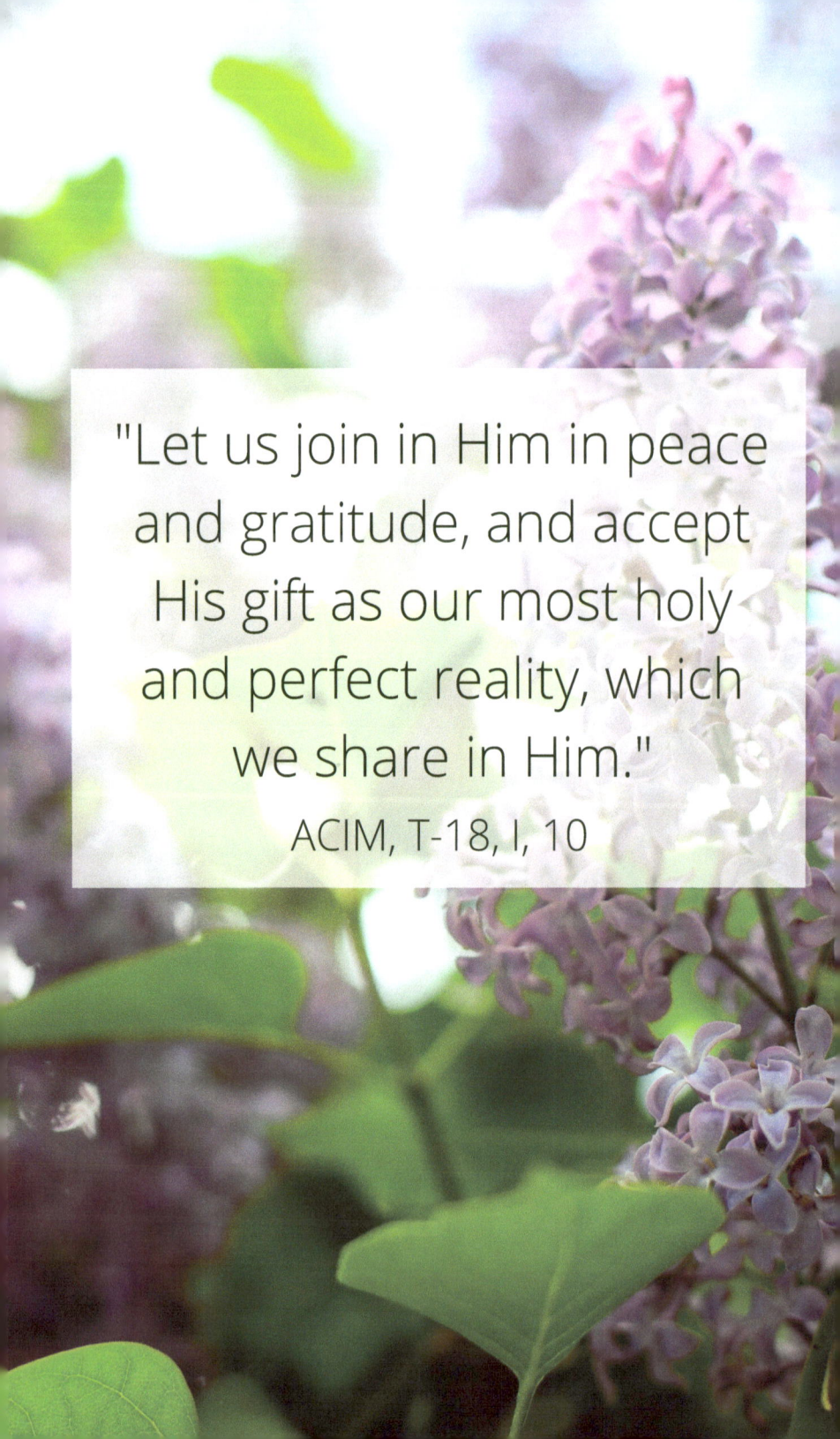

Holy Spirit

I offer thanks to God, our Father, today
That in me, all things will find their freedom

In my gratitude to God
I make room for all who will escape with me

I thank my Father today
I rejoice today
That no exceptions can ever be made
That will reduce my wholeness

Amen

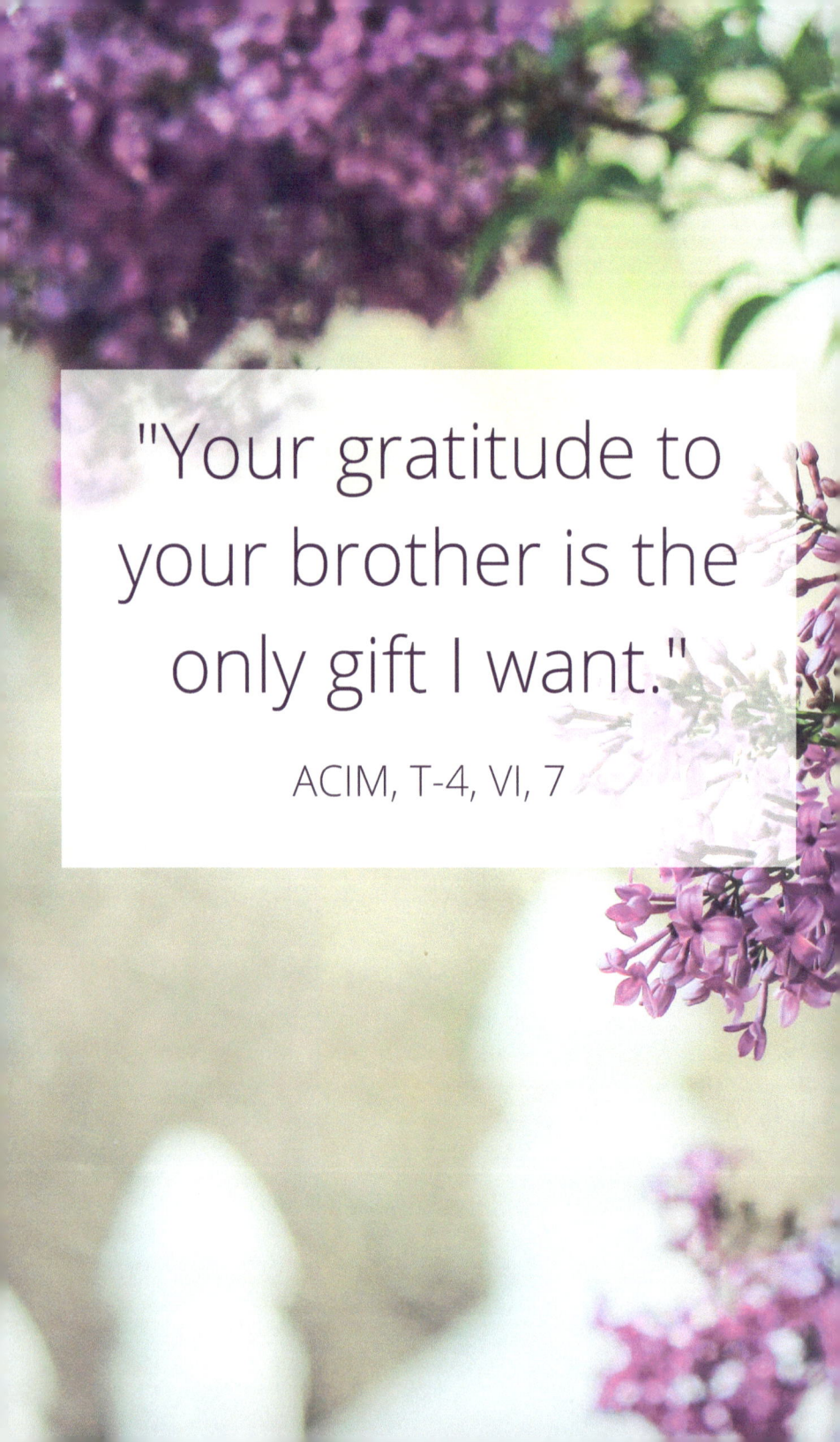

"Your gratitude to your brother is the only gift I want."

ACIM, T-4, VI, 7

I thank you, Father

For these holy ones
Who are my brothers
As they are your Sons

My faith in them is yours
I offer them the gift
Of your eternal gratitude

I will to do
Only your Holy Will
And give eternal thanks
For the loveliness
That is them
Amen

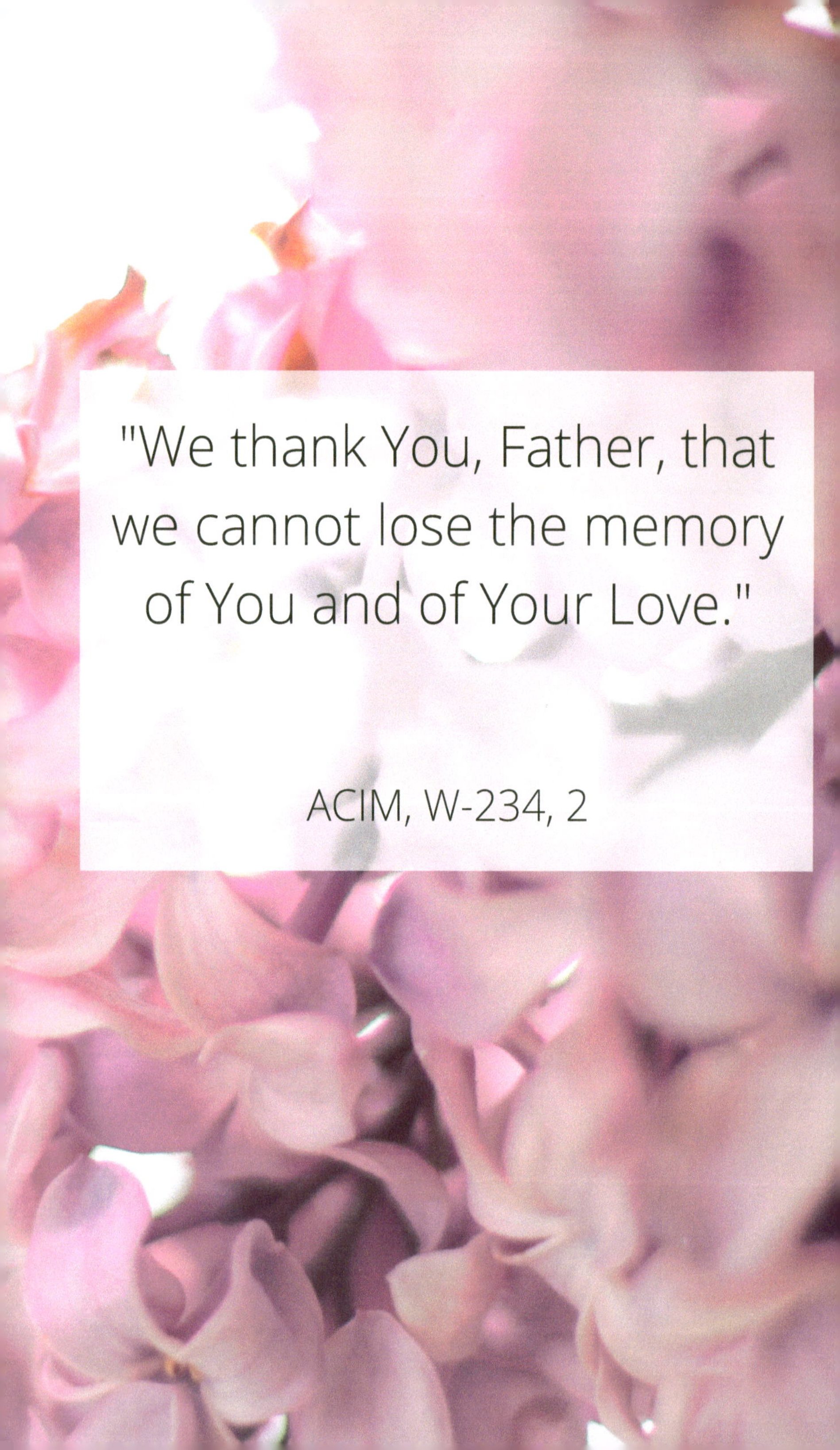

"We thank You, Father, that we cannot lose the memory of You and of Your Love."

ACIM, W-234, 2

Holy Spirit

Peace be with me today
And to all my brothers

How grateful am I for God
The One I never separated from
The One Whom I am One with always
The One whom I am in now

My mind is part of God's
I am very Holy
Let me not forget this
Amen

"Let us wait here in silence, and kneel down an instant in our gratitude to Him Who called to us and helped us hear His Call."

ACIM, C - Ep, 4

Holy Spirit

Bless this moment

Bless it with me

As I fall into you

And lose all of me

In you

There are no cares

There are no worries

Only perfect calm

Into your Eternal peace

I enter now

I fly on the wings of an eagle

High above the nothingness

That once was a battleground

Amen

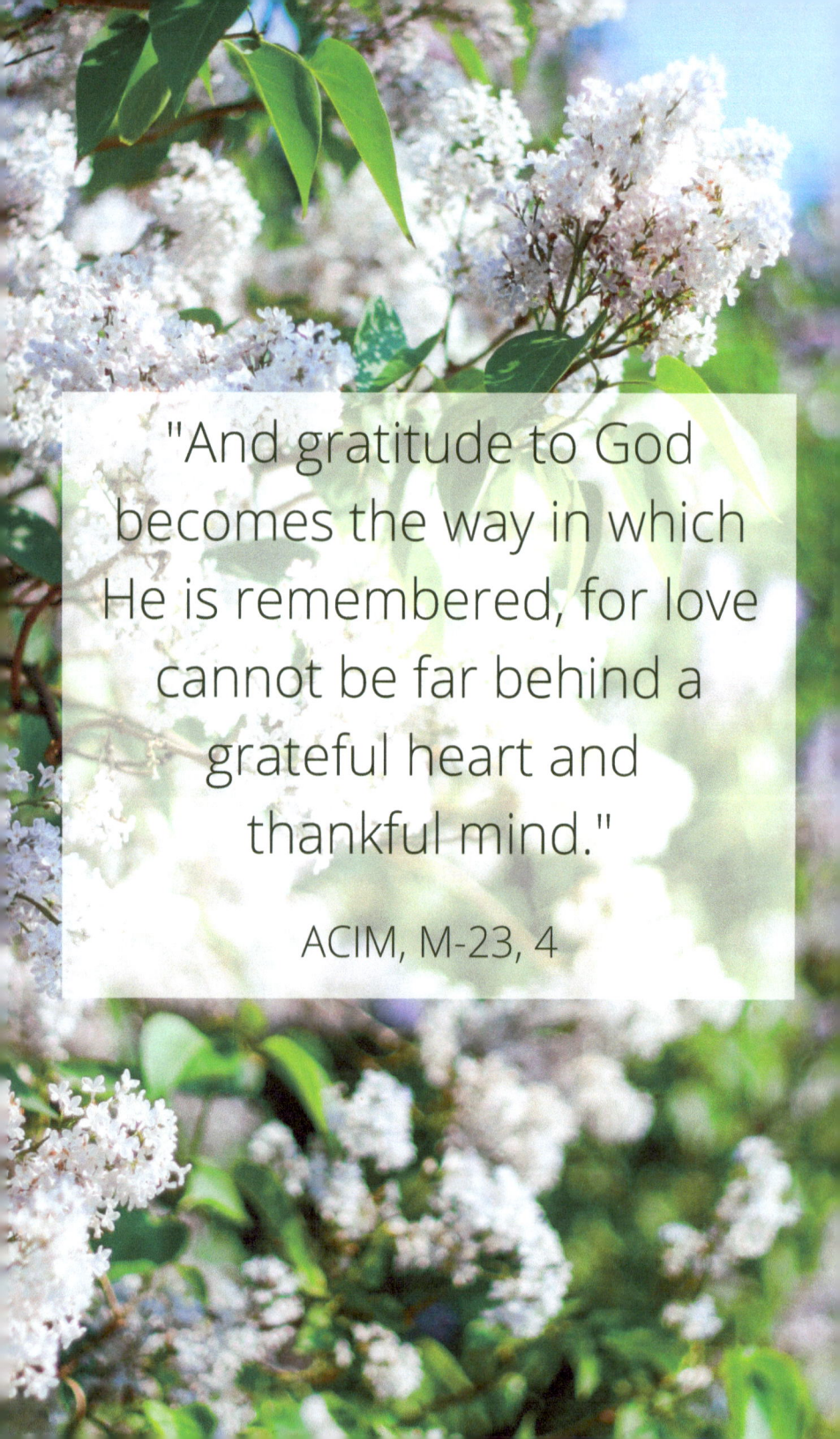

DEAR HOLY SPIRIT

Thank you for always being with me

Thank you for being in my mind

Thank you for helping me see differently

Thank you for helping me see Peace instead of this

Thank you for always being the loving

Words and wisdom

That speak to me

You never judge or criticize me

I trust in your guidance

You are my trusted inner Friend

Amen

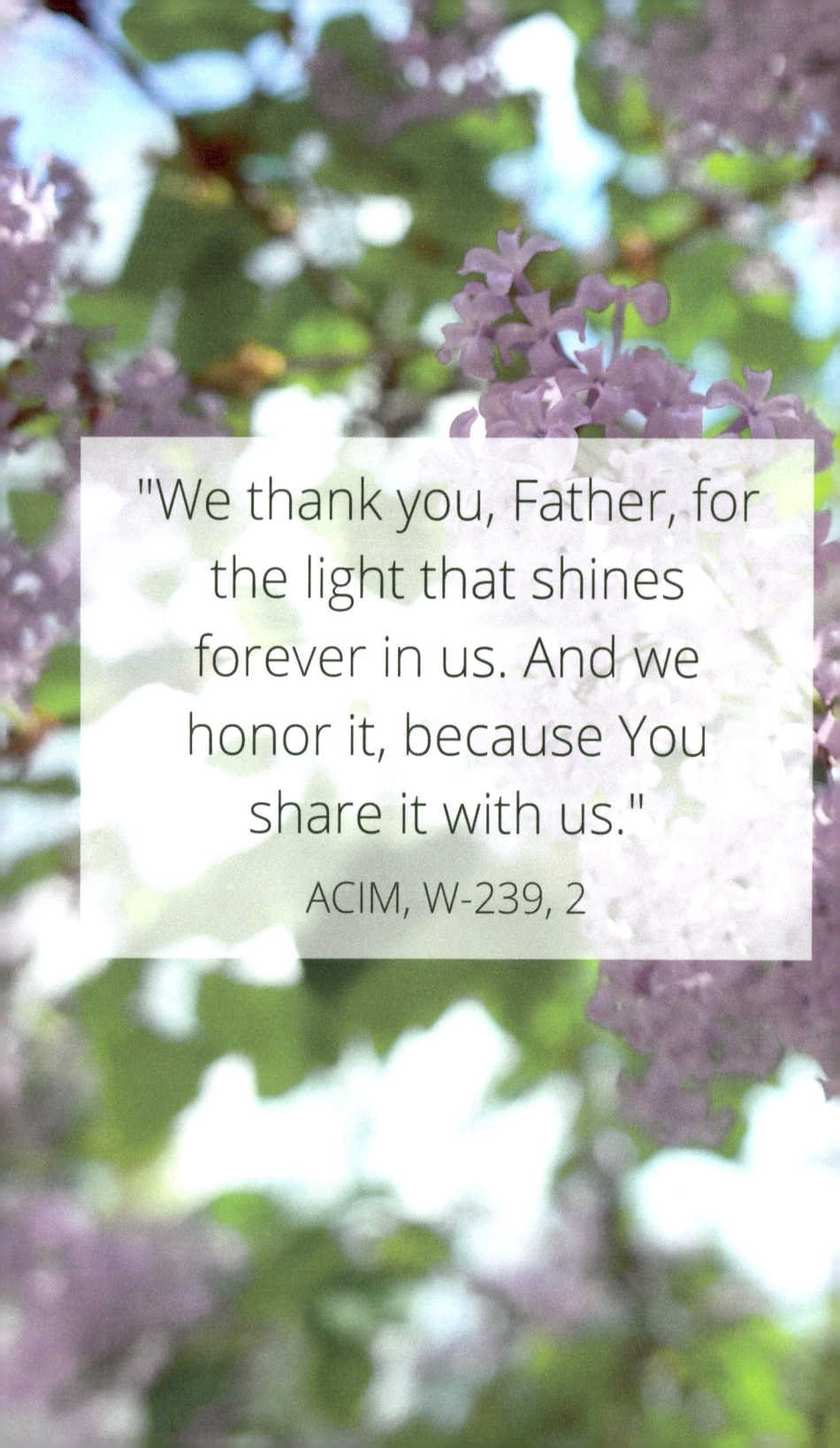

Holy Spirit

You are my right Mind

You are the Holy Mind in which

All God's thoughts reside

Ideas leave not their source

I reside as a holy idea

A Holy Thought

In the Mind of God

I am grateful for this understanding

Of where I really am

Amen

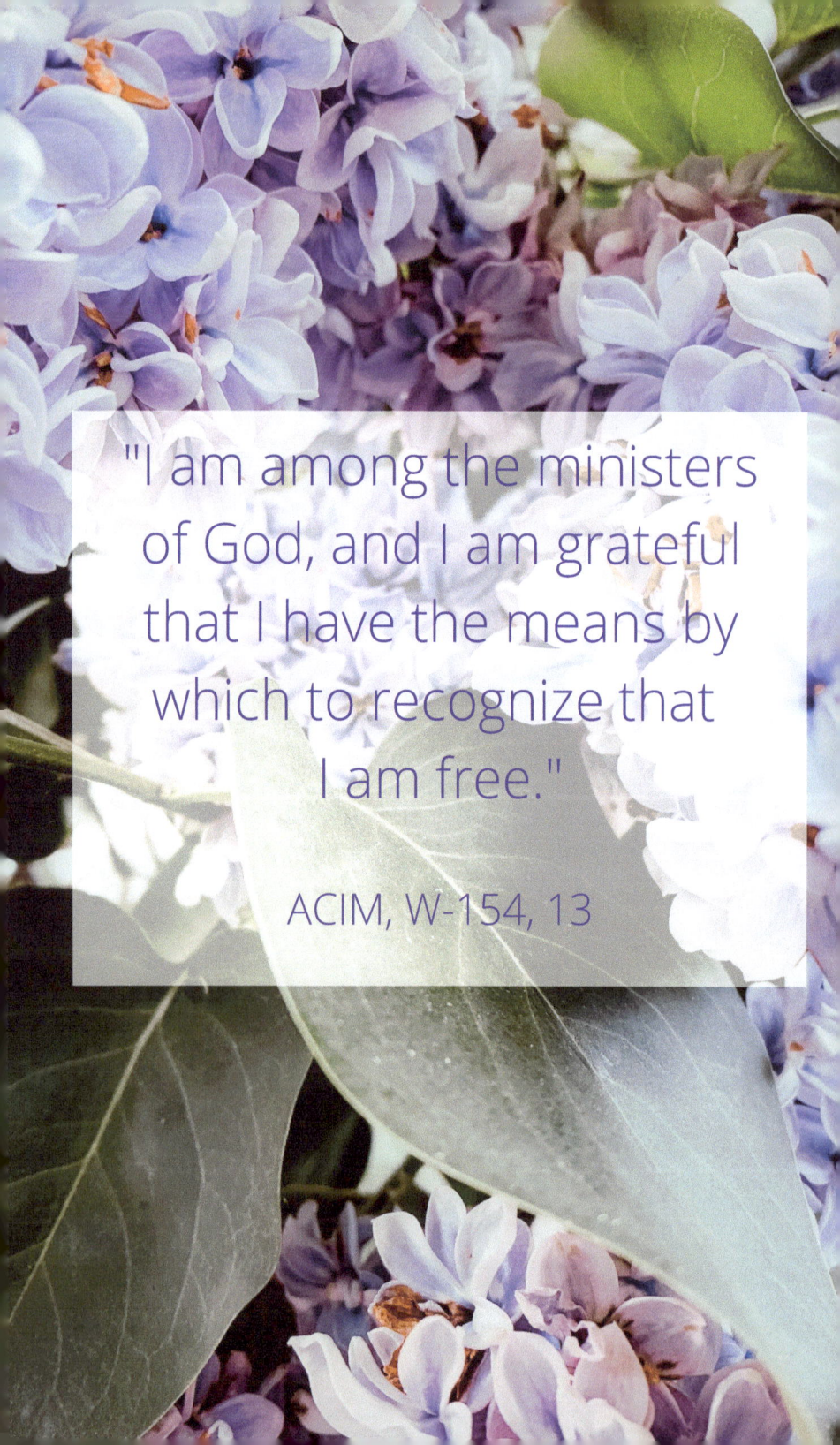

"I am among the ministers of God, and I am grateful that I have the means by which to recognize that I am free."

ACIM, W-154, 13

Holy Spirit

I am truly grateful

To experience the Love that I am

A love beyond measure

I am truly grateful

For bringing your peace and joy

To all around me

I am truly grateful

To know God's spirit of perfect Love

As my Self

I am deeply grateful

For the lessons you help me learn

Which teach me

That I am Love

Amen

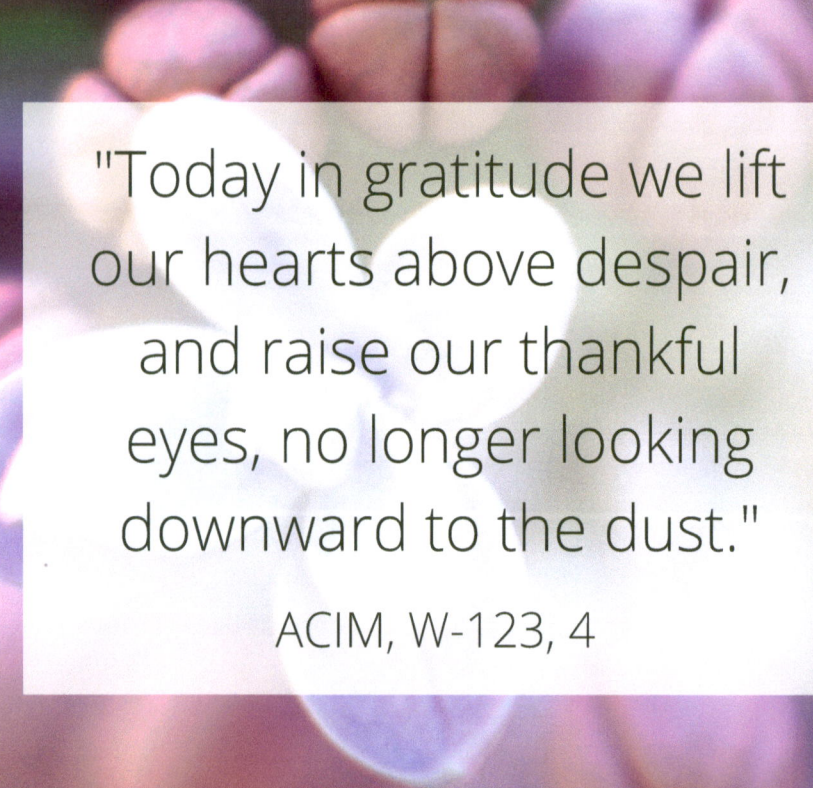

"Today in gratitude we lift our hearts above despair, and raise our thankful eyes, no longer looking downward to the dust."

ACIM, W-123, 4

Holy Spirit

My only desire is

To see everything and everyone

As you see them

Through God's perfect Vision

I am grateful

To have the vision of Love

Lift me out of sorrow

I am grateful

For having A Course in Miracles

To light my way

I am truly grateful

I can now perceive

From blessings of holiness

Amen

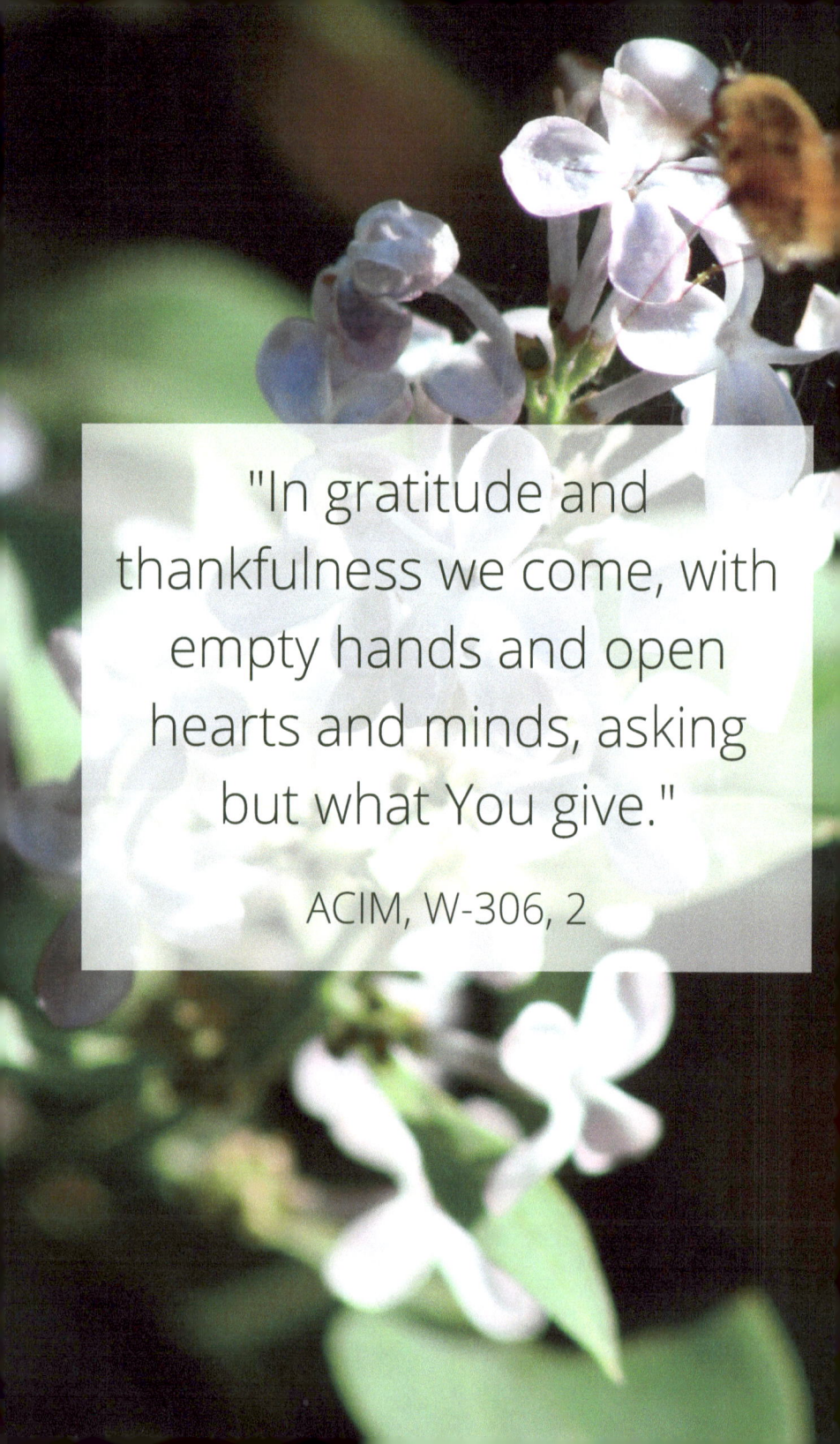

"In gratitude and thankfulness we come, with empty hands and open hearts and minds, asking but what You give."

ACIM, W-306, 2

Holy Spirit

I hear your eternal call
Of love that never ends
It sings a song that is all
Of love that is beyond

I sit and sing with you
A song with notes so lovely
Notes that don't exist here
In time and space and form

I lift myself and join
In the endless song of joy
The song that sings of endless love
The song of endless gratitude
The notes that play forever
In your holy Mind of Love

Amen

"And as we gather miracles from Him, we will indeed be grateful. For as we remember Him, His Son will be restored to us in the reality of Love."

ACIM, W-350, 2

Holy Spirit

I am blessed by every beneficent thought

Of any of my brothers, anywhere

I want to bless them in return

Out of gratitude

Please be the Mind in which I bless

In which I extend your holy instant

In which I extend your Infinite Love

In which my gratitude blesses them

And my holiness shines brightly

As I see with True Vision

The perfect Christ before me

Amen

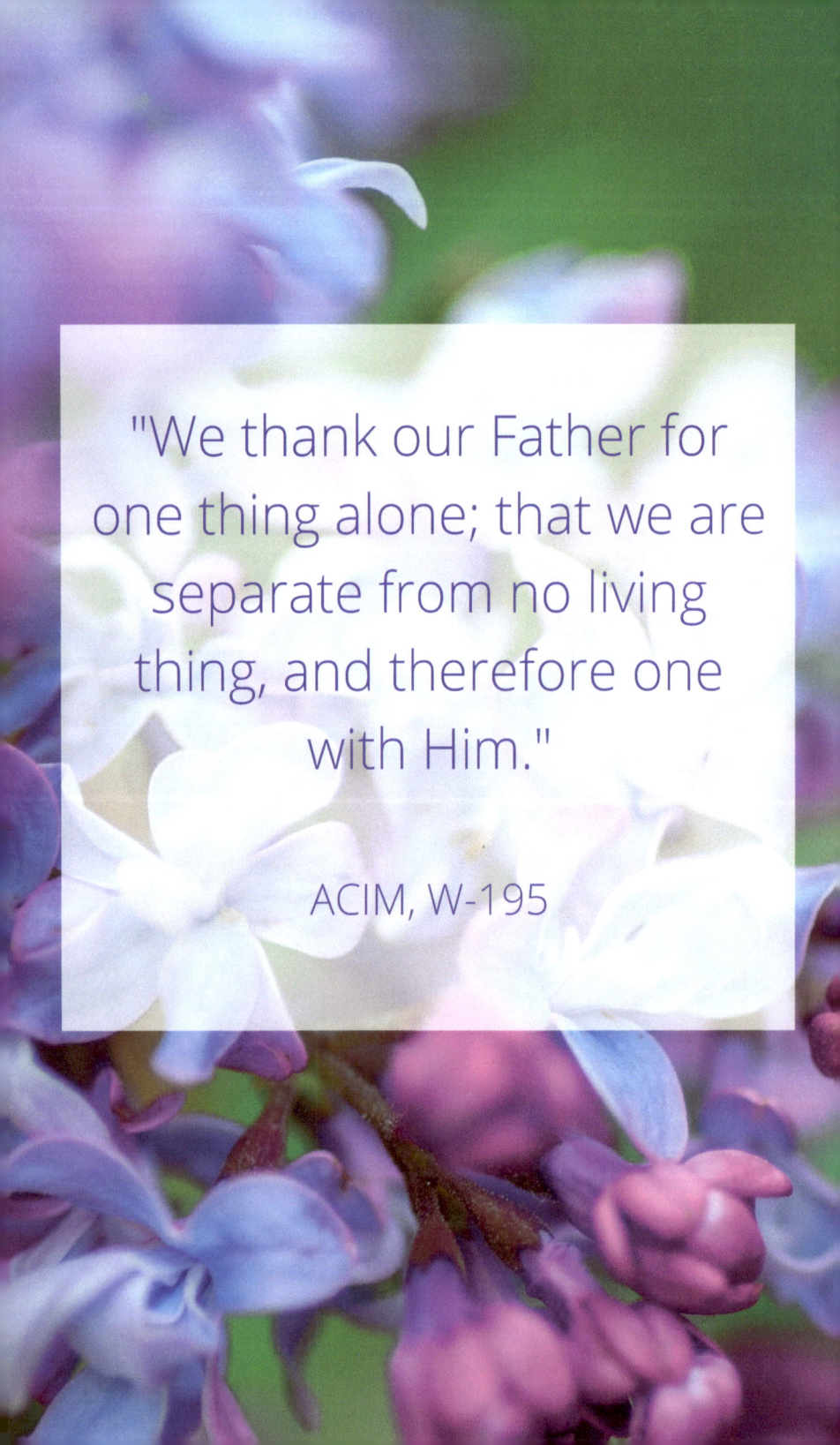

THANK YOU, GOD

Thank you, Father

Thank you for your peace today

You are One Mind that sees no differences

The One Mind that sees my brother as my Self

One Son

One Sonship

In the everlasting Mind of God

I feel myself now

In Your Unceasing Love

A Holy Love that I have my being in

As I remain always

Amen

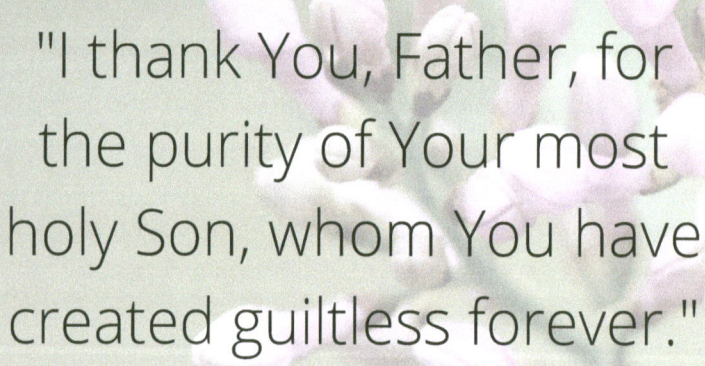

"I thank You, Father, for the purity of Your most holy Son, whom You have created guiltless forever."

ACIM, T-13, X, 12

Dearest Father

Thank you for giving me

Your Spirit

Your Mind

Your Thoughts

So that I can move out of the mind of fear

That I can move out of the ego's

Limiting thoughts and beliefs

And move into your mind of eternal Love

Into eternal Life

A mind and heart of open Love

I immerse myself

And am filled with Your Love and Peace

Amen

Father

As my heart joins yours

As your heart joins mine

We join in this song of Love

Beyond the world

Calling and singing to each other

In the most joyous rapture

Beyond all thinking

Beyond words and concepts

Is this song of Songs

I hear you sing to me

In endless peace

In endless joy

Calling my name

Where there are no names

The notes oh so beautiful

The joyful love Song

Within

I am lifted up

Into Your eternal heart

In gratitude

Lost in your Love

Amen

"Where sin once was perceived will rise a world that will become an altar to the truth, and you will join the lights of Heaven there, and sing their song of gratitude and praise."

ACIM, T-26, IV, 5

Holy Spirit

Deep gratitude to you
My dear friend
Of love and life and joy

I am deeply grateful
For your guidance
And loving wisdom

Please choose for God for me
Please decide for me
Please respond for me
Be in my mind today

Help me remember to ask
For your loving guidance
In all moments
In gratitude and love
Amen

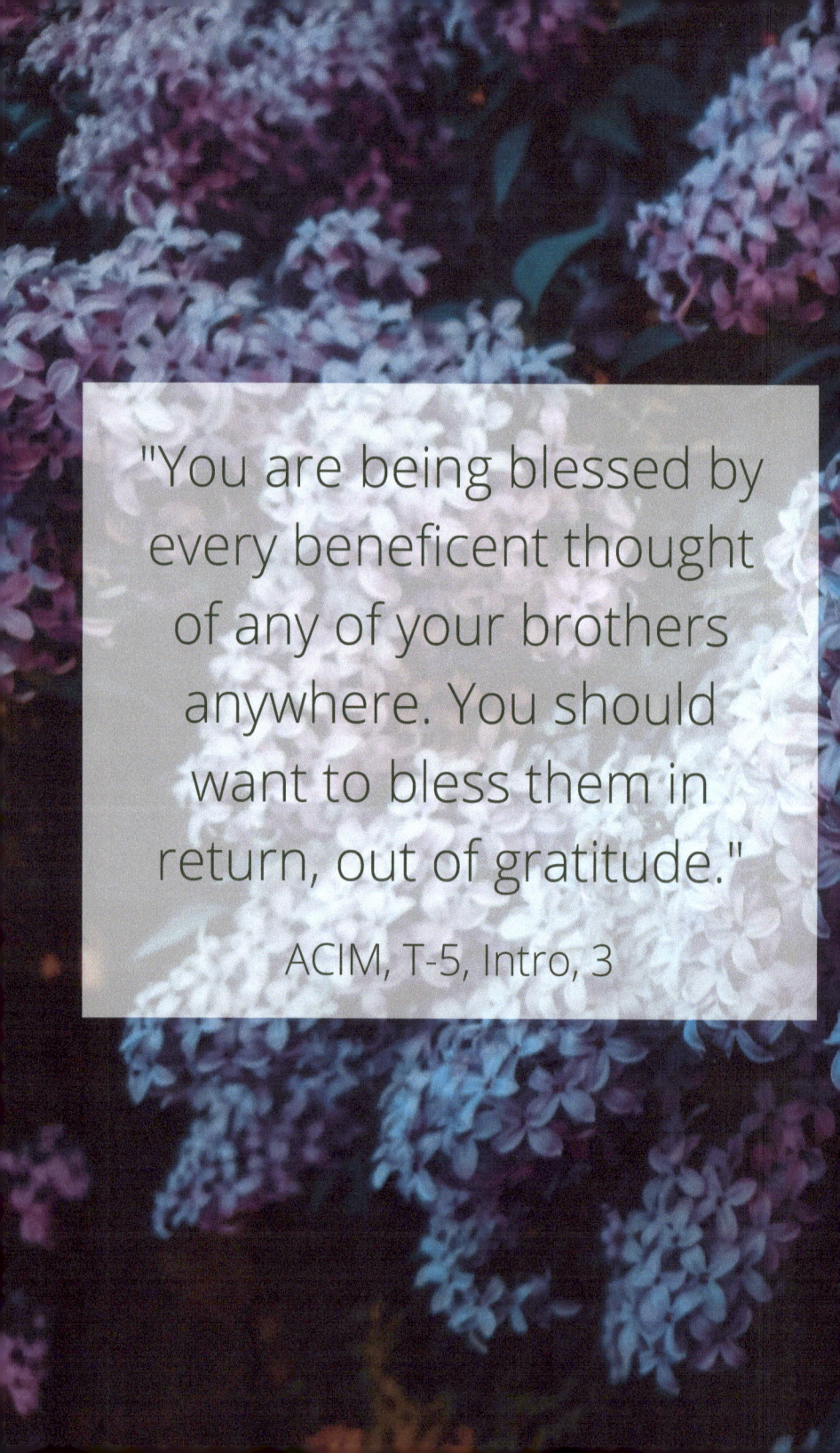

Holy Spirit

You ask me only for gratitude

Towards my brother

You tell me that it is the only gift

That you want from me

If I am grateful to my brother

I am really expressing gratitude to God

For what He created

And in my gratitude

I come to know my brother

As he was created

Wholly perfect and innocent

The Perfect Christ Self

And this is all I want to behold

In the loving light of truth

Amen

"Through your gratitude you come to know your brother, and one moment of real recognition makes everyone your brother because each of them is of your Father."

ACIM, T-4, VI, 7

HOLY SPIRIT

I want only to bless
My brother with gratitude
I need not know them individually
To have them be at effect
Of my loving gratitude

You tell me that my light is so strong
That it radiates throughout the Sonship
And blesses all creation
And returns thanks to the Father

I bless all now with my holiness
And feel gratitude returned to me
Today I learn the lesson
That giving is receiving
Amen

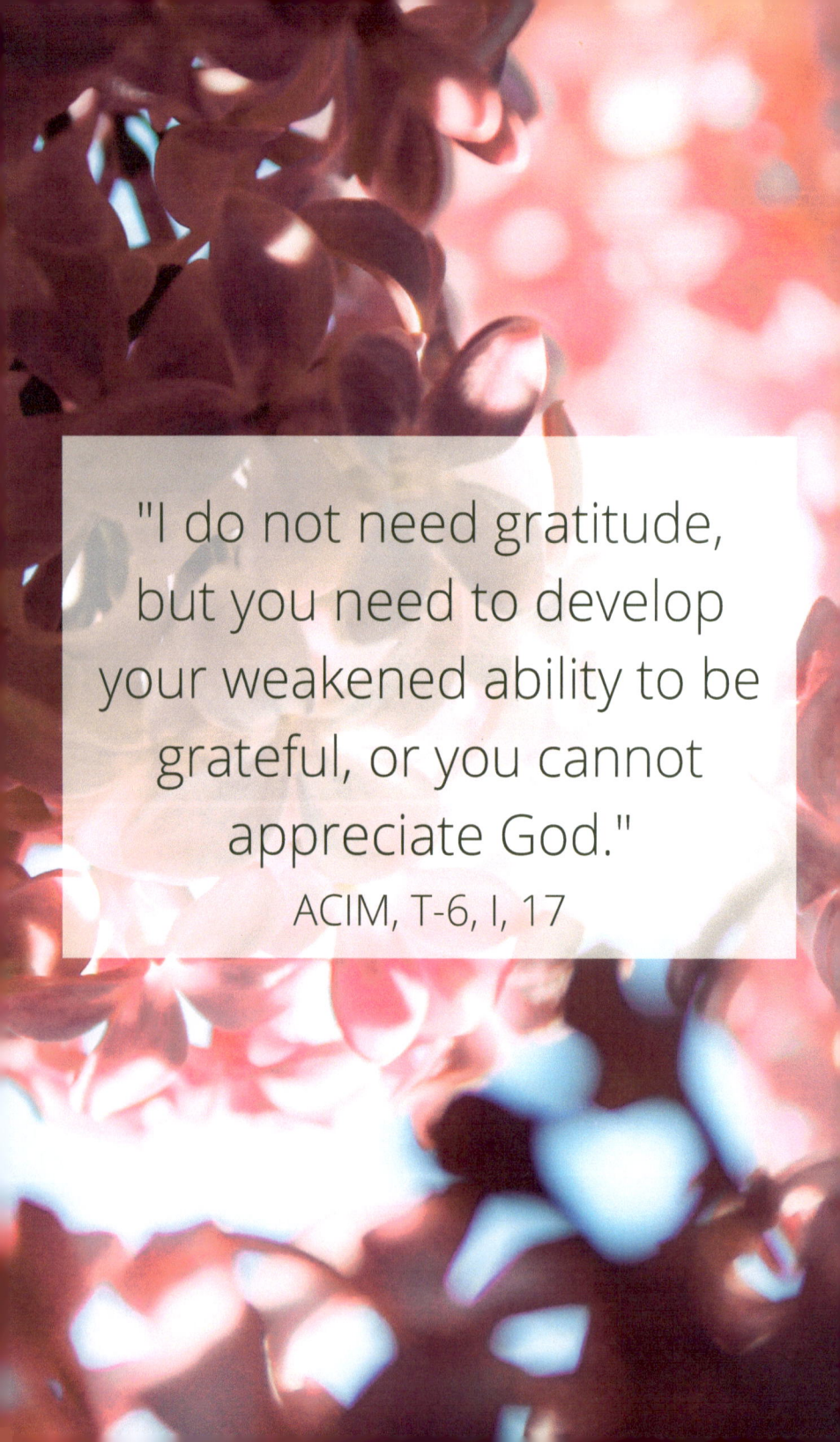

"I do not need gratitude, but you need to develop your weakened ability to be grateful, or you cannot appreciate God."

ACIM, T-6, I, 17

Today I learn to think of gratitude

In place of anger, malice and revenge.

I learn that I have been given everything

And thus gratitude

Becomes the single thought

I will substitute

For my insane perceptions

I will listen for God calling me

And answer with a heart full

Of thankfulness

Amen

"Join, then, with me in praise of Him and you whom He created. This is our gift of gratitude to Him, which He will share with all His creations, to whom He gives equally whatever is acceptable to Him."

ACIM, T-8, IV, 7

Holy Spirit

My gratitude will pave the way

To knowledge of my Self

I choose to have time shortened

By accepting that gratitude and love

Bring me closer to the time

When separation has an ending

God gives thanks to me today

For being what I am

My gratitude to God

Is the only road to Him

Amen

"In gentle gratitude do God the Father and the Son return to what is Theirs, and will forever be."

ACIM, T-26, IX, 8

Gratitude remains part of Love

The two go hand in hand

I remind myself that my thankful heart

Leads me unto God's love

I feel its blessing upon my heart

I feel it lifting me above the world

I feel raised up and interwoven

With a love blessed and draped

In gratitude to all everywhere

Amen

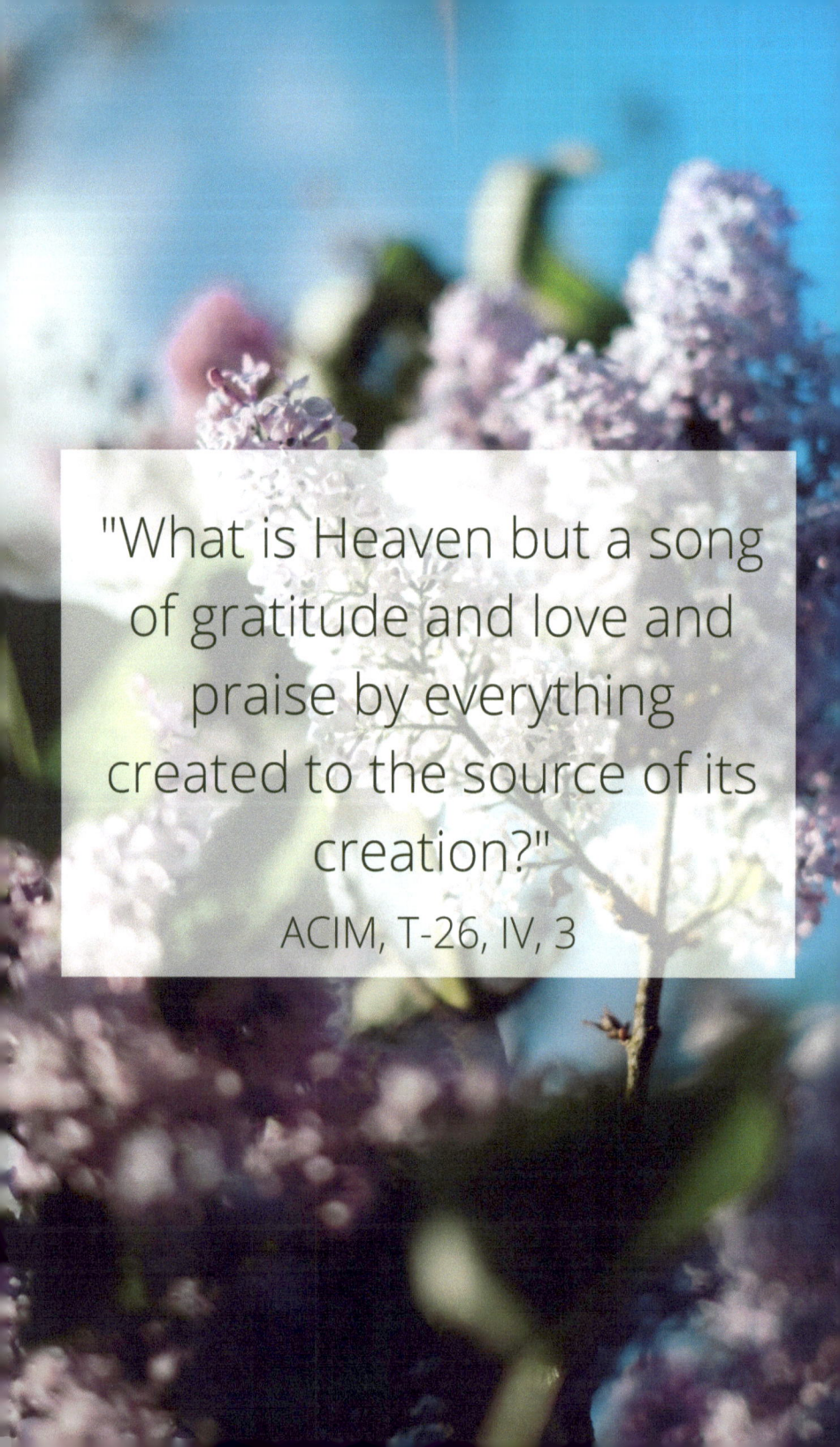

"What is Heaven but a song of gratitude and love and praise by everything created to the source of its creation?"

ACIM, T-26, IV, 3

Thanks be to you
Holy Son of God
Today I thank my brother
For helping me awaken to my Self
We walk together
Hand in hand
We cannot enter Heaven apart
We are all together
In the song of songs
Singing in gratitude and love
To our Holy Father
How glorious the sounds
How glorious the gratitude
That lifts us up
And melts us together
Into the Holy Heart of Love
Amen

"All things that live bring gifts to you, and offer them in gratitude and gladness at your feet. The scent of flowers is their gift to you. The waves bow down before you, and the trees extend their arms to shield you from the heat, and lay their leaves before you on the ground that you may walk in softness, while the wind sinks to a whisper around your holy head."

ACIM, W-156, 5

Holy Spirit

I accept God's gift to me today

Of His gratitude of my creation

I accept God's gift to me today

Of His most gracious Love

I let go of everything

That is not of divine Will

And know I need do nothing

But let Him in

To show me the way

To my Self

Amen

Dearest brother, we offer you this Christ blessing

I love you

I bless you

I honor you

You are guiltless

You are innocent

You are sinless

You are perfect

You are whole

You are complete

You are the Holy Christ

Your worth is established by God

Love,

Cate & Shannon

About the Author

In January 2015, after a two-year deep immersion with the teachings of *A Course in Miracles* and joining with the Holy Spirit and Jesus to undo the split mind, Cate's mind awakened to the infinite, vast, eternal, boundless, all-encompassing Love that is. In that moment, a download of understanding of the Course's teachings entered her mind and a knowing became clear that "God is in everything I see because God is in my mind". Cate's mind entered the Song of Heaven, where perfect Oneness sang the most beautiful song of love and gratitude.

On New Years Day 2016, the Holy Spirit showed Cate a picture of the cover of a Holy Spirit prayer book and guided her to start writing these prayers down. Over time, the prayers were divided by themes from *A Course in Miracles* and a flower background design was given for easy recognition to the theme. These prayer books are here to be helpful for any mind that wishes to know how to "pray". Forgiveness prayer is to invite the Hoy Spirit in, ask Him for help to see our brother or the situation differently and then wait for His beautiful loving answer to enter our mind.

The Holy Spirit's purpose for these prayers, is to "Let these prayers nourish the desert of the unawakened mind with the living waters of God's Love".

To find out more about Cate, visit: categrieves.com

About the Designer

In December of 2020, Shannon was guided to support Cate in all things. This book is one of the many ways she is so honored to serve and it has been a beautifully divine experience playing her part in following guidance on the design of this prayer book. Shannon is filled with gratitude to be of service to Him, to Cate and to all of her brothers to be truly helpful in all ways.

Shannon has been *A Course in Miracles* student since 2009 and joined with Jesus quickly to learn his Course. After two years of practicing ACIM and relying on Jesus to guide her, bringing in miracles, shifting her perception from fear to love, Shannon was pulled outside of time and space. She realized that where she was, is what she is. She experienced freedom from everything she once believed and it continues to bring the experience of beauty, in every moment.

To find out more about Shannon, visit: thehappylearners.com

www.ingramcontent.com/pod-product-compliance
Lightning Source LLC
Chambersburg PA
CBHW041403090426
42743CB00006B/146